Night Life in Bangkok
The Wild Side of Thailand

Arthur Crandon LL.B. (Hons.) M.A.

Night Life in Bangkok – The Wild Side of Thailand

Copyright Arthur Crandon 2024

All rights reserved. No part of this book may be reproduced, stored in a retrieval system, or transmitted in any form or by any means—electronic, mechanical, photocopying, recording, or otherwise—without the prior written permission of the publisher, except for brief quotations in critical reviews or articles.

This is a work of fiction. Names, characters, places, and incidents are either the product of the author's imagination or used fictitiously. Any resemblance to actual persons, living or dead, events, or locales is entirely coincidental.

ISBN: 9798340197191

Cover design by Lynnie Ceniza
Interior design and formatting by Lynnie Ceniza
Published by Arthur Crandon Publishing
Visit our website: Arthurcrandon.co.uk

DISCLAIMER

The information provided in this book is for general informational purposes only. It does not constitute legal, financial, or professional advice. While every effort has been made to ensure accuracy, the author and publisher assume no responsibility for errors or omissions. Readers should consult with appropriate professionals for specific advice tailored to their individual circumstances.

First Edition: August 2024

Remember, my friend, these cocktails aren't just drinks; they're time machines. Each sip carries echoes of bygone eras, whispered secrets, and the clinking of glasses across centuries. So next time you're at Q&A Bar, raise your glass and toast to the past, the present, and the magic in between!

Let's embark on a moonlit adventure through the vibrant tapestry of Bangkok's nightlife. Whether you're craving rooftop views, pulsating dance floors, or a rendezvous with street food, I've got you covered. So grab your imaginary fedora (because every adventurer needs one) and let's dive in

CONTENTS

	Acknowledgments	i
1	Famous Places to Visit	1
2	Romantic Adventures	11
3	Floral Themed Cafes	23
4	Instagram	29
5	Cocktail Bars	35
6	Unusual Place	41

Remember, my adventurous friend, the Cocktail Journey isn't just about sipping; it's about storytelling. Each drink carries whispers of distant lands, forgotten ballrooms, and clandestine meetings. So go forth, collect stamps in your cocktail passport, and may your taste buds dance like tango partners under the moonlight!

1 FAMOUS PLACES TO VISIT

Khao San Road

Khao San Road—the legendary thoroughfare where the night wears its dancing shoes, and adventure beckons from every neon-lit corner! Allow me to whisk you away to this vibrant slice of Bangkok's nightlife, where the air hums with excitement and the moon winks knowingly.

Why Is Khao San Road Famous? Khaosan Road isn't just a street; it's a living, breathing entity—a kaleidoscope of energy, backpacker tales, and sensory overload. Let's unravel its secrets:
1. **The Backpacker Mecca**: Once upon a time (and still today), Khaosan Road was the pilgrimage site for backpackers. They'd arrive, dusty and wide-eyed, fresh from

temples up north or beach parties down south. It's where travel stories were swapped over cheap beers and pad thai.
2. **The Neon Symphony**: Neon signs flicker like fireflies, spelling out promises of adventure. The air vibrates with laughter, music, and the clinking of glasses. You'll hear snippets of conversations in a dozen languages—French, German, Spanish, and the universal language of wanderlust.
3. **Cocktail Buckets and Nitrous Balloons**: Oh, the concoctions! Picture oversized buckets filled with colorful potions—vodka, fruit juices, and a dash of mischief. And those nitrous balloons? A quick inhale, and suddenly the world tilts just right.
4. **Street Food Extravaganza**: Hunger strikes? Fear not. Street food vendors line the road, offering everything from mango sticky rice to fried insects. Grab a plastic stool, balance your plate, and savor the chaos.

Is It Worth Visiting? Absolutely! Khaosan Road is a sensory carnival, and here are some gems to explore:

1. **Rocco Club**: Impossible to miss, Rocco Club stands tall at the entrance. It's a 6-story complex with rooftop vibes, pool

tables, and two clubs. Start with sunset drinks on the rooftop, then descend for late-night revelry.
2. **Mischa Cheap / Tropical Galaxy**: These bars are like old friends—reliable, unpretentious, and ready to serve you a cold one. Sidle up, order a Singha beer, and people-watch.
3. **SUP DUDE**: The name alone invites curiosity. SUP DUDE is where you'll find backpackers swapping stories, playing beer pong, and dancing barefoot.
4. **The One Khao San Center**: A maze of bars, live music, and backpacker camaraderie. Grab a bucket, join the dance floor, and let the night unfold.
5. **Empire Bar**: It's like stepping into a vintage postcard. Swing seats, fairy lights, and reggae tunes. Order a mojito, sway to the rhythm, and pretend you're in a Hemingway novel.
6. **The Club Khaosan**: When the clock strikes midnight, head here. The bass thumps, the crowd pulses, and inhibitions dissolve. Dance like nobody's watching (because they're too busy dancing too).

Dos and Don'ts on Khaosan Road:
- **Dos**: Smile, chat with strangers, try weird street food, and embrace the chaos.
- **Don'ts**: Don't be overly cautious; let

spontaneity guide you. And avoid the overly aggressive tuk-tuk drivers—they're like Bangkok's unofficial rollercoaster operators.

Best Hotels Nearby:
- **The Siam Hotel**: Luxurious riverside retreat.
- **Riva Surya Bangkok**: Affordable elegance.
- **Tales Khaosan – Cafe & Hostel**: Budget-friendly and buzzing.

So, my fellow night owl, slip into your dancing shoes, let the neon guide you, and may your Khaosan nights be filled with laughter, serendipity, and memories that glow brighter than the streetlights!

Enchanting Rooftop Bars

Let's elevate our spirits (both metaphorically and literally) as we explore Bangkok's enchanting rooftop bars.

1. **CRU Champagne Bar**:
    - **Location**: Perched on the circular 59th floor atop Centara Grand at CentralWorld.
    - **Vibe**: A 360° panoramic view of

Bangkok awaits you. The elegant white furniture, the shimmering lights—it's a scene straight out of a movie.

- **What to Expect**: CRU Champagne Bar focuses on premium champagnes and signature cocktails. Imagine sipping bubbly while the city sprawls beneath you.
- **Atmosphere**: DJs spin tunes, and the convivial coolness sets the tone. It's a place where celebrations come alive against the glittering skyline.
- **Hours**: Open daily from 17:00 to 01:00. Last order at 00:30.
- **Dress Code**: Smart casual—dress to impress! No tank tops, shorts, or flip-flops allowed.
   Signature Drink: Try their Hangovertini—a nod to *The Hangover* fame.

2. **Lennon's at Rosewood Bangkok**:

   - **Location**: On the top 30th floor of Rosewood Bangkok.
   - **Vibe**: A stylishly moody speakeasy inspired by a '70s-era home recording studio. Think vinyl

records, rare spirits, and cigars.
- **Unique Feature**: An interactive 6,000-vinyl collection—the largest in Asia. Play your favorite tunes and sip signature cocktails.
- **Hours**: Open daily from 18:00 to midnight.
- **Dress Code**: Smart casual—appropriate attire and closed footwear.

3. **Sky Bar at Lebua State Tower**:

    - **Location**: Suspended 820 feet in the air, it's one of the highest rooftop bars globally.
    - **Scene**: Made famous by *The Hangover*, this iconic spot offers 360-degree views of Bangkok's skyline.
    - **Bar Magic**: The LED-lit cylindrical bar changes colors every 90 seconds.
    - **Cocktails**: Classic and offbeat concoctions—perfect for capturing memories and Instagram-worthy moments.
    - **Hours**: Open daily from 17:00 to midnight.
    - **Dress Code**: Dress your best—no

athletic wear or flip-flops allowed.

So, whether you're humming the James Bond theme or channeling your inner rockstar, these rooftop bars promise unforgettable nights. Cheers to sipping and soaring above the City of Angels!

Dance Floors to Visit

Let's turn up the volume, sync our heartbeat to the bass, and explore Bangkok's electrifying dance floors.

1. **Levels Club & Lounge:**
    - **Location:** Situated in the heart of Bangkok, Sukhumvit area, Levels Club & Terrace hosts a world-class nightlife experience. Picture an amazing audio-visual environment where beats collide with luxury table service.
    - **Music:** Levels Club brings international resident DJs, star guest DJs, and themed event nights. From house to hip-hop, they've got your rhythm covered.
    - **Dress Code:** Dress to impress! Leave the flip-flops, hoodies, and

sportswear at home. This is your moment to shine.
- **Hours:** From 9 pm until late—because the night is young, and the dance floor awaits!

2. **Beam:**
    - **Location:** Beam is an honest club with a communal vibe, located at 72 Courtyard, Sukhumvit Soi 55 (Thonglor).
    - **Vibe:** Expect precise music policy, an ear-shifting sound system, and brain-mess visuals. It's where freedom meets phenomenal music.
    - **Music Genres:** Beam features different music genres on each level. House/techno DJs take over the Dalmatian Room, while hip-hop rules the main room.
    - **Drinks:** The bar offers more than 20 new drinks, including Beam's signature cocktails, shooters, and buckets. Cheers to dancing the night away!

3. **Sing Sing Theater:**
    - **Location:** Nestled in Thonglor, Sing Sing Theater is a cinematic, retro-futuristic chinoiserie den. Imagine Shanghai in the 1930s colliding with Blade Runner aesthetics.

- **Décor:** Metalwork, wood, lanterns, and neon lights create an otherworldly atmosphere. The dance floor pulses, and gimmicky performances unfold.
- **Drinks:** Try the Cabinet Escape (served in a birdcage) or the Bank in Lemon (a Thai twist on a classic gin drink).
- **Balcony View: The second-floor balcony offers the best spot for enjoying the shows.**

So, my fellow dance deity, pick your stage, let the music guide you, and may your nights in Bangkok be a symphony of beats, laughter, and unforgettable connections!

2 ROMANTIC ADVENTURES

Let's set sail on the Chao Phraya River, where enchantment meets cuisine, and the cityscape becomes our backdrop.

Chao Phraya River Dinner Cruise Highlights:

1. **The Setting**:
    - Imagine stepping aboard a beautifully adorned riverboat. The Chao Phraya River, also known as the "River of Kings," flows through the heart of Bangkok. As you glide along, the city's iconic landmarks—illuminated against the night sky—paint a magical tableau.

2. **Authentic Thai Cuisine**:
   - The dinner buffet onboard offers a delightful array of authentic Thai dishes. From fragrant curries to spicy salads, you'll taste the rich flavors of Thailand. And yes, Pad Thai—the quintessential Thai noodle dish—is likely part of the feast.
3. **Live Music and Entertainment**:
   - As you dine, a live band sets the mood. Their melodies blend with the gentle lapping of water against the boat. It's like having your own private concert under the stars.
4. **Wat Arun and the Grand Palace**:
   - Keep your camera ready! The silhouette of Wat Arun (Temple of Dawn) and the majestic Grand Palace—both beautifully lit—will steal your breath. These iconic landmarks tell tales of centuries past.
5. **Romantic Vibes**:
   - Whether you're celebrating an anniversary, a honeymoon, or simply a special night out, the Chao Phraya River cruise adds a touch of romance. Candlelight, soft music, and the gentle sway of the boat—it's

a fairy tale come true.
6. **No Midnight Pumpkin Transformation**:
    - Fear not! Unlike Cinderella, you won't turn into a pumpkin at midnight. Instead, you'll disembark with memories etched in starlight.

Practical Details:
- **Duration**: Typically 2 to 2.5 hours.
- **Pickup Option**: Some cruises offer hotel pickup for convenience.
- **Price**: Around ฿1,400 per person (includes Indian buffet, cruising time, live singing, water, and Indian masala tea).

So, my fellow dreamer, step aboard, clink glasses, and let the Chao Phraya weave its magic. May your night be as enchanting as a moonlit serenade!

Bangkok Tree House

Let's delve into the enchanting world of the **Bangkok Tree House** and its captivating "View with a Room" experience—a true escape from the bustling city into a serene, starlit haven.

1. **The Concept**:
   - The Bangkok Tree House is an eco-friendly boutique hotel nestled in the green lung of the city. It's a place where sustainability meets romance, and nature embraces luxury. Imagine being cocooned in a treetop nest, surrounded by mangrove palms and the gentle sounds of the river.
2. **View with a Room**:
   - **Rate**: The "View with a Room" experience costs 4,000 THB on weekdays and 4,500 THB on holidays (per night, for 2 guests).
   - **Accommodation**: You'll stay in a unique top-floor viewing platform—an open-air "nest" perched 20 feet above the ground. It's like having your own private skybox with uninterrupted views of the Chao Phraya River.
   - **Setting**: The bed inside the mosquito net allows you to sleep under the stars. Imagine stargazing together, feeling the gentle breeze, and being serenaded by nature.
   - **Contingency Plan**: Don't worry about rain or insects; they've got it

covered. You'll be comfortable and cozy, even if the weather surprises you.
3. **Romantic Shots and Memories**:
    - Whether you're celebrating a special occasion or simply seeking a romantic escape, the "View with a Room" promises unforgettable moments. Capture unique shots against the night sky, share whispered conversations, and create memories that glow brighter than the stars.
4. **Contact Details**:
    - **Address**: 60 Moo1, Petchaheung Rd soi 26, Bang Nampeung, Phra Pradeang, Samutprakarn, Bangkok, 10130
    - **Phone**: 082-995-1150 / 085-845-7666
    - **Social Media**: Find them on Facebook (@bangkoktreehouse) and Instagram (bangkoktreehouse).

Remember, this isn't just a hotel; it's an invitation to disconnect, reconnect, and fall in love all over again. So, my fellow stargazer, may your night at the Bangkok Tree House be filled with celestial magic and whispered promises!

Themed Cafes and Restaurants

Let's embark on a delightful journey through Bangkok's themed cafés and restaurants—each one a little universe of its own. Whether you're a cat lover, a rooftop enthusiast, or simply seeking an Instagram-worthy spot, these places promise memorable experiences.

1. **Caturday Cat Café**:
    - **Location**: Hidden away in the charming neighborhood of Ari, Caturday Cat Café is a '50s diner-themed haven with a nostalgic twist. Imagine stepping into a neon-lit interior reminiscent of shows like *Riverdale* or *Stranger Things*. The black-and-white checkered floors, old-school posters, and retro vibes set the stage.
    - **Menu**: Indulge in milkshakes, burgers, and deep-fried sides served on vintage plates. Try their California Cheeseburger (฿190) and pair it with a Hazelnut Milkshake (฿165). Perfect for snapping

Instagram-worthy pics with their signature milkshakes—just like Archie or Betty!
- **Address**: 25 Ari 4 Fang Nua Alley, Samsen Nai, Phaya Thai, Bangkok 10400
- **Opening Hours**: 11 am to 8 pm daily
- **Nearest BTS Station**: Ari
- **Tip**: Make a reservation to secure your spot in this retro time capsule!

2. **Above Eleven Rooftop Bar**:
   - **Location**: Perched on the 33rd floor of Fraser Suites Sukhumvit, Above Eleven offers breathtaking views of Bangkok's skyline. It's a unique Peruvian rooftop experience with zesty pisco sours, epic sunsets, and vibrant Peruvian-Japanese cuisine.
   - **Menu**: Explore Nikkei Cuisine—a fusion of Japanese and Peruvian influences. Savor dishes like sushi classics, ceviche, and more. And don't miss their signature cocktails—Pisco Sours and Japanese fusions.
   - **Entertainment**: Dance the night away to live tunes, salsa nights, and

rotating DJs. It's the hottest rooftop bar in town!
    - **Address**: 33rd Floor, Fraser Suites Sukhumvit, Sukhumvit Soi 11, Khlong Toei Nuea, Watthana, Bangkok 10110
    - **Opening Hours**: 6 pm to 2 am daily
    - **Dress Code**: Dress to impress—no sandals or flip-flops allowed!
    -
3. **Other Themed Gems**:
    - Don't miss Trok Khrut Café (a hidden gem), Ha Tien Café (with European influences), and Floral Café at Napasorn (for a garden escape). Each one has its own charm and story waiting to unfold.

So, my fellow café explorer, pick your theme, sip your coffee, and let the magic of Bangkok's themed spots whisk you away!

1. **Trok Khrut Café**:

    - **Location**: Trok Khrut Café is tucked away in the historic neighborhood of Phra Nakhon. Its unassuming entrance leads to a cozy oasis.
    - **Atmosphere**: The café exudes retro

vibes with vintage furniture and an eclectic mix of décor. It's like stepping into a time capsule.
- **Menu**: Enjoy a mid-priced menu with a variety of options. Try their salted edamame or indulge in a heaping sundae glass of coconut ice cream with mango on top.
- **Address**: 58 Khrut Alley, Khwaeng Sarn Chao Phho Sua, Khet Phra Nakorn, Bangkok 10200
- **Opening Hours**: Daily from 09:30 to 21:00
- **Contact**: +66 86 413 8352
- **Review**: Visitors praise the excellent service, good food, and engaging interior design. It's a place where creativity meets comfort.

2. **Ha Tien Café**:

   - **Location**: Ha Tien Café is situated on Maha Rat Road, near the Grand Palace. It's a hidden gem waiting to be discovered.
   - **Setting**: The café occupies an old shophouse and is adorned with antique wooden furniture. The chocolate carrot cake and cheesecake are highly

recommended.
   - **Address**: 4 Maha Rat Rd, Khwaeng Phra Borom Maha Ratchawang, Khet Phra Nakhon, Bangkok 10200
   - **Opening Hours**: Daily from 10:00 to 18:00
   - **Contact**: +66 81 302 0651
   - **Review**: Visitors appreciate the elegant atmosphere and superb cakes. Don't miss this gem if you're in the area!

3. **Floral Café at Napasorn**:

   - **Location**: This café is a floral delight located on Chakphet Road near the Bangkok Flower Market (Pak Khlong Talat).
   - **Ambiance**: The café is on the second floor above a flower studio. Dangling foliage crawls over brick walls, and an elaborate chandelier adds to the charm.
   - **Menu**: Enjoy coffee, teas, cakes, and a light menu. The raspberry chocolate rose cake and raspberry rose ice cream are must-tries.
   - **Address**: 67, Chakphet Road Wang Burapha Phirom, Phra Nakhon, Bangkok 10200

- **Opening Hours**: Daily from 09:00 to 19:00
- **Contact**: +66 99 468 4899
- **Review**: Visitors describe it as a masterpiece of creative decor—a place where love for flowers and aesthetics come together. 🌸 🍰

So, whether you're seeking nostalgia, elegance, or floral enchantment, these cafés promise delightful experiences. Choose your favorite and let the cozy corners tell their stories!

3 FLORAL THEMED CAFES

1. **Trok Khrut Café**:

    - **Location**: Trok Khrut Café is tucked away in the historic neighborhood of Phra Nakhon. Its unassuming entrance leads to a cozy oasis.
    - **Atmosphere**: The café exudes retro vibes with vintage furniture and an eclectic mix of décor. It's like stepping into a time capsule.
    - **Menu**: Enjoy a mid-priced menu with a variety of options. Try their salted edamame or indulge in a heaping sundae glass of coconut ice cream with mango on top.

- **Address**: 58 Khrut Alley, Khwaeng Sarn Chao Phho Sua, Khet Phra Nakorn, Bangkok 10200
- **Opening Hours**: Daily from 09:30 to 21:00
- **Contact**: +66 86 413 8352
- **Review**: Visitors praise the excellent service, good food, and engaging interior design. It's a place where creativity meets comfort.

2. **Ha Tien Café**:

    - **Location**: Ha Tien Café is situated on Maha Rat Road, near the Grand Palace. It's a hidden gem waiting to be discovered.
    - **Setting**: The café occupies an old shophouse and is adorned with antique wooden furniture. The chocolate carrot cake and cheesecake are highly recommended.
    - **Address**: 4 Maha Rat Rd, Khwaeng Phra Borom Maha Ratchawang, Khet Phra Nakhon, Bangkok 10200
    - **Opening Hours**: Daily from 10:00 to 18:00
    - **Contact**: +66 81 302 0651
    - **Review**: Visitors appreciate the

elegant atmosphere and superb cakes. Don't miss this gem if you're in the area!

3. **Floral Café at Napasorn**:

    - **Location**: This café is a floral delight located on Chakphet Road near the Bangkok Flower Market (Pak Khlong Talat).
    - **Ambiance**: The café is on the second floor above a flower studio. Dangling foliage crawls over brick walls, and an elaborate chandelier adds to the charm.
    - **Menu**: Enjoy coffee, teas, cakes, and a light menu. The raspberry chocolate rose cake and raspberry rose ice cream are must-tries.
    - **Address**: 67, Chakphet Road Wang Burapha Phirom, Phra Nakhon, Bangkok 10200
    - **Opening Hours**: Daily from 09:00 to 19:00
    - **Contact**: +66 99 468 4899
    - **Review**: Visitors describe it as a masterpiece of creative decor—a place where love for flowers and aesthetics come together.

So, whether you're seeking nostalgia, elegance, or floral enchantment, these cafés promise delightful experiences. Choose your favorite and let the cozy corners tell their stories!

Whether you're a flower lover, an Instagram enthusiast, or simply seeking a cozy escape, these cafés promise delightful experiences:

1. **Kinn Kaffe & Craft**:

    - **Location**: Nestled in Chatuchak, Kinn Kaffe & Craft is a coffee lover's dream. Their brews are delicious, and they pair perfectly with their selection of yummy cakes.
    - **Signature Drink**: Try the "Romeo & Juliet"—their signature drink that comes with a KitKat! And don't miss their Coconut Cake made with real coconut meat.
    - **Interior**: The café's interior is equally delightful, with an array of cozy spots to choose from. It's like a coffee-scented wonderland. ● 🌿
    - **Address**: 6/22, Soi Ladprao 25, Chan Kasem, Chatuchak, Bangkok 10900,

2. **Floral Cafe @ Napasorn**:

- **Location**: Hidden near Bangkok's famous 24-hour flower market, this secret gem houses an enchanting floral space. The café changes its floral decor according to the four seasons, so every visit feels fresh and magical.
- **Interior**: From every corner, your eyes will feast on stunning floral arrangements. It's like stepping into a blooming fairy tale.
- **Address**: 67 Chakkraphet Rd, Wang Burapha Phirom, Phra Nakhon, Krung Thep Maha Nakhon 10200, Thailand

3. **Baker x Florist**:

   - **Location**: Drop by Rama 9 lane, and you won't miss Baker x Florist—the café facade is adorned with beautiful floral arrangements.
   - **Cosy Picnic Vibes**: Imagine having a little picnic with your girlfriends amidst all the blooms. Sip on their Autumn Branch latte or Ruby Rose mocktail while enjoying Salmon Steak Caper Sauce with Mashed Potatoes.

- **Don't Miss**: Their delectable cakes—they're as pretty as the flowers!
- **Address**: 66 Rama 9 Soi 41, Suan Luang, Bangkok 10250, Thailand

So, my fellow bloom enthusiast, pick your favorite spot, inhale the floral scents, and let the petals weave their magic.

4 INSTAGRAM

Cafés are like little havens of inspiration, and capturing Instagram-worthy shots there can be both fun and rewarding. Whether you're a seasoned café hopper or just starting your coffee adventure, here are some tips to make your café photos pop on the 'gram:

1. **Order photo-ready food and drink combinations:**
    - Nobody wants to double-tap a boring food or drink item. Keep it interesting! Start by photographing a beautiful subject. Lattes are always a safe bet, especially if the café is known for unique latte art. Look for special ingredients—maybe there's a lavender latte or a Turkish coffee pour-over on the menu. Unique elements catch viewers' attention and make them engage with your image.
2. **Rearrange the scene if you're with more**

than one person:
- Variety is key! If you're at a café with friends or family, play around with different compositions. Move cups, plates, and utensils to create diverse shots. The more options you have, the better chance you'll find the perfect image.

3. **Wait for the right time of day:**
- Natural light is your best friend. Early mornings or late afternoons often provide soft, flattering light. Avoid harsh midday sun—it can cast unflattering shadows. Sit near a window or choose an outdoor seat if possible.

4. **Find the best light:**
- Look for soft, diffused light. If you're indoors, sit near a window or under an umbrella if you're outside. Backlit shots can create a dreamy effect, especially when capturing steam rising from a cup of coffee.

5. **Choose your location wisely:**
- Not all cafés are created equal in terms of aesthetics. Seek out cafés with interesting interiors, unique decor, or cozy corners. Vintage furniture, plants, and textured walls make great backgrounds.

6. **Experiment with angles:**
- Don't settle for the usual straight-on shot. Try overhead shots (flat lays) of your table setup, or capture details like latte art from a

lower angle. Shoot from different sides to see what works best.
7. **Be mindful of distractions:**
   o Before clicking, scan your frame for distracting elements. Remove clutter, stray napkins, or other people's belongings. Keep the focus on your subject—the coffee, pastry, or cozy ambiance.

Remember, café photos are about more than just coffee; they tell stories of relaxation, connection, and indulgence. So sip your latte, soak in the atmosphere, and let your creativity flow!

Bangkok, with its vibrant energy and diverse landscapes, offers numerous Instagram-worthy spots that will make your feed pop. Whether you're into historic temples, futuristic architecture, or chic cafes, there's something for everyone. Let's explore some of the most photogenic places in Bangkok:

1. **The Grand Palace and Wat Phra Kaew:**
   o The Grand Palace is an iconic Bangkok attraction. Its intricate architecture, golden spires, and vibrant colors make it a must-visit. Don't miss Wat Phra Kaew (Temple of the Emerald Buddha) within the

palace complex—it's a photographer's dream. Remember to dress modestly when visiting temples!

2. **Wat Arun (Temple of Dawn):**
   - Wat Arun, with its stunning riverside location, is especially magical during sunrise or sunset. Climb its steep steps for panoramic views of the Chao Phraya River and the city skyline.
3. **Wat Benchamabophit (The Marble Temple):**
   - This temple, made entirely of Italian marble, is a serene oasis. The white facade against blue skies creates a beautiful contrast. Visit early in the morning for soft light and fewer crowds.
4. **Loha Prasat at Wat Ratchanatdaram:**
   - Loha Prasat, also known as the Metal Castle, is a unique iron temple. Its intricate design and symmetry are perfect for architectural shots. Visit during the day or at night when it's beautifully lit.
5. **Chinatown (Yaowarat):**
   - Explore the bustling streets of Chinatown. Capture vibrant street

scenes, neon signs, and food stalls. The chaos and colors make for dynamic photos.

6. **Asiatique The Riverfront:**
   - This open-air mall along the Chao Phraya River offers great views of the city. Visit during the evening for the Ferris wheel and the illuminated letters spelling "Asiatique."

Rooftop Bars:

7. Bangkok's skyline is best appreciated from rooftop bars. Try Sky Bar at Lebua State Tower (made famous by *The Hangover*), Above Eleven, or CRU Champagne Bar. Sip cocktails while the city lights twinkle below.
8. **Artbox Bangkok:**
   - If you're lucky to visit during Artbox (a pop-up market), you'll find colorful shipping containers, street art, and quirky installations. It's a feast for the eyes!
9. **Floral Cafés:**
   - Cafés like Baker x Florist and Floral Café @ Napasorn offer beautiful floral backdrops. Sip coffee surrounded by blooms and capture

those cozy moments.
10. Street Art in Bangrak and Charoenkrung:
- Explore these neighborhoods for vibrant murals, graffiti, and creative street art. The walls tell stories and add character to your photos.

Remember, the best shots often come from unexpected corners. So keep your camera ready, explore with curiosity, and let Bangkok's charm unfold through your lens! Happy snapping

..

5 COCKTAIL BARS

Let's delve deeper into these covert corners of Bangkok:

1. **Q&A Bar**:
    - Imagine stepping into a vintage train carriage, the air thick with nostalgia. Q&A Bar, tucked away in Asoke, invites you to board the "Bangkok Express." Each cocktail is a card in your journey—a passport stamp for your taste buds. Dress sharp, sip thoughtfully, and let the candlelight reveal mysteries.
    - **Address**: 235/13 Soi Sukhumvit 21, Khlong Toei Nuea, Watthana, Bangkok 10110, Thailand
    - **Opening Hours**: Tuesday-Sunday, 6pm-12am (Closed on Mondays)

2. **Havana Social**:
    - A secret alley on Sukhumvit 11 leads to 1940s Cuba. Dial the code, step through the phone booth, and emerge in Havana Social. The air hums with Latin rhythms, and mojitos flow freely. You're part of a covert salsa mission—sip, sway, and let the night unravel.
    - **Location**: Somewhere between intrigue and rhythm.
3. **Iron Balls Distillery**:
    - Not Narnia, but close. Find the photo booth, pull the lever, and enter a gin lover's paradise. Iron Balls crafts spirits like alchemical potions. The ambiance? Dark, mysterious, and perfect for plotting adventures. Capture it all in a snapshot.
    - **Address**: 18/1 Sukhumvit 45, Khlong Tan Nuea, Watthana, Bangkok 10110, Thailand
4. **Rabbit Hole**:
    - Fall down this rabbit hole in Thonglor. Bartenders here are magicians, turning spirits into liquid gold. Order the "Mad Hatter's Elixir" and let whimsy guide your night.
    - **Location**: Somewhere between

reality and dreams.
5. **Tep Bar**:
    - Venture to the old town, where Tep Bar awaits. It's a revival of Thai drinking culture. Wooden decor, live music, and herbal-infused concoctions set the scene. Try their "Ya Dong" shots—a sip of liquid folklore. 🌿 🖼 🎶
    - **Address**: 69-71 Soi Nana, Pom Prap, Pom Prap Sattru Phai, Bangkok 10100, Thailand

Remember, these aren't just bars; they're portals to stories waiting to unfold. Decode the secrets, sip the elixirs, and may your nights be as mysterious as a locked diary!

1. **The Passport**: First, you'll need your metaphorical passport. Purchase a little book—the kind that holds secrets and dreams. This isn't your average passport; it's a ticket to flavor destinations.

2. **The Deck of Cards**: Imagine a deck of cards, each featuring a classic cocktail. These cards aren't for poker; they're your compass. Each card points to a different libation—a sip of history, a swirl of creativity. Shuffle them like a seasoned traveler preparing for an adventure.

3. **Four Cocktails to Begin**: Your journey begins with four cocktails. These aren't mere drinks; they're chapters in your cocktail novel. Sip, savor, and let the flavors transport you. Maybe you'll start with an Old Fashioned—the timeless classic that whispers of gentlemen in fedoras and secret rendezvous. Or perhaps a Sidecar—the elegant concoction that waltzed through Parisian nights.

4. **Destination Unknown**: As you progress, explore beyond the familiar. Maybe you'll encounter a Corpse Reviver #2 (don't worry, it won't actually revive any corpses)—a zesty elixir with gin, Cointreau, and a dash of absinthe. Or perhaps a

Sazerac—the New Orleans legend that dances with rye whiskey and bitters. Each cocktail is a waypoint, a marker on your map.

6 UNUSUAL PLACES

Bangkok's nightlife is a vibrant tapestry of sensory delights, and there are plenty of unique experiences waiting to be discovered after the sun sets. Let's dive into some of the most unusual and captivating things you can do in this electric city at night:

1. **Dine Inside an Airplane at Chang Chui Night Market**:
    - Imagine having dinner inside a decommissioned Lockheed L-1011 TriStar airplane! At **Chang Chui**

Plane Night Market, you can do just that. This market is a blend of art, food, and fantasy. The main attraction, **Na-Oh Bangkok**, takes dining to new heights (literally). Local ingredients shine in dishes that are both simple and sophisticated.

- But it's not just about the food—the entire market buzzes with creativity. You'll find quirky shops, live music, and intriguing art installations. The airplane itself sits at the heart of it all, promising an otherworldly meal. Choose between a 5-course or 8-course menu, where each dish tells a story of Thailand's rich culinary landscape.

Explore Unique Bars with Crazy Cool Interiors:

- Bangkok is home to some seriously funky bars. From live jazz music to mind-bending interiors, each spot has something special to offer. Here are a few that caught my eye:

- **Iron Fairies**: This whimsical bar feels like stepping into a fairy tale. It's adorned with iron sculptures, dim lighting, and an enchanting atmosphere.
- **Tep Bar**: For a taste of traditional Thai culture, head to Tep Bar. It's all about vintage vibes, live music, and herbal-infused cocktails.
- **Maggie Choo's**: Located in a former bank vault, Maggie Choo's blends jazz, burlesque, and Asian-inspired decor. It's mysterious and utterly captivating[2].

Roof-Top Revelry and Sky Bars:

- Bangkok's skyline is dotted with rooftop bars that offer breathtaking views. Places like **Vertigo and Moon Bar** (at Banyan Tree Hotel) or **Octave Rooftop Lounge &**

Bar (at Marriott Hotel) let you sip cocktails while gazing out over the city lights. It's a magical experience that shouldn't be missed.

Street Food Adventures:
- While not entirely unusual, Bangkok's street food scene is legendary. Venture into the bustling night markets—like **Asiatique the Riverfront** or **Talad Rot Fai Ratchada**—and sample everything from spicy papaya salad to mango sticky rice. The combination of flavors, aromas, and the lively atmosphere is unforgettable.

Hidden Gems and Speakeasies:
- Bangkok has its fair share of secret bars tucked away in unexpected places. Seek out spots like **Rabbit Hole** or **Find the Photo Booth** (yes, it's hidden behind a photo booth curtain) for a clandestine evening of mixology and intrigue.

Remember, Bangkok doesn't just wake up at night—it comes alive. Whether you're dancing until dawn, savoring street eats, or exploring hidden corners, this city's nocturnal scene is a testament to its endless energy. So go ahead, feel the pulse of Bangkok after dark—it's a journey you won't soon forget!

Visit Arthurcrandon.co.uk for More Titles

Retirement to the Philippines
K1 Fiance visa to the U.S. – Fast Track
Secrets to buying Condos in the Philippines
Buying Land in the Philippines
Annulment in the Philippines
Breaking free from a bad marriage
Get a visit visa to America First time
Marriage in the Philippines
Get a visit visa to the United Kingdom
Ghosts, Spectres, and folklore in the Philippines
Retiring to Spain – a Comprehensive Guide
Spousal Visa to America
Spousal visa to the United Kingdom
Working in the UK.
Working in the US.

ABOUT THE AUTHOR

Arthur Crandon is a retired lawyer and a prolific writer. He is British and grew up in a rural community in Somerset. He has lived in England, Wales, Hong Kong and the Philippines and now spends most of his time in the Philippines with his Visayan wife and their son.

He loves to hear from anyone who has anything to do with the Philippines – you can email him anytime on:

ac@arthurcrandon.co.uk

www.ingramcontent.com/pod-product-compliance
Lightning Source LLC
Chambersburg PA
CBHW030051230526
45471CB00003B/1042